Original title:
Between the Doors and the Window

Copyright © 2025 Creative Arts Management OÜ
All rights reserved.

Author: Harrison Blake
ISBN HARDBACK: 978-1-80587-063-0
ISBN PAPERBACK: 978-1-80587-533-8

Treading the Line of Awareness

Thoughts bounce like a ball,
Chasing shadows on the wall.
One foot in reality,
The other in my dreams, you see.

Doodling lines with my toes,
Wobbling like a jester's pose.
Is it real or just a dance?
I laugh at every chance.

The Crossing of Unknowns

A leap of faith, a little jig,
An awkward spin, oh so big!
With every step, I think of snacks,
Crossing unknowns requires some hacks.

The grass looks green, or maybe blue,
Who knew colors could confuse, too?
With each twist around this bend,
I smile wide, because it's pretend.

Stirrings in the Gloom

In the dark, where giggles hide,
A tickle monster won't abide.
It lurks behind the curtains drawn,
Hatching laughter at the dawn.

I tiptoe soft on squeaky floors,
Hoping to avoid the snores.
A dance-off with the shadows there,
Who wins? Oh, that's a real scare.

Spaces Between the Beats

I bop my head, I tap my feet,
In between, there's quite a beat.
Pause for snacks, then groove again,
This rhythm makes me feel like a hen.

Skip a dance, then pull a face,
Each step a game, a wacky chase.
I laugh, I spin, and twirl around,
In the space, pure joy is found.

Secrets Behind the Barrier

There's a cat with a plan, oh so sly,
Sneaking snacks that just fly by.
Behind the wall, its antics unfold,
In corners where no one is told.

A mystery wrapped in a fur ball,
Knocking plants down as they fall.
It giggles and darts with such glee,
A shadow that dances, carefree.

Caught in the Interstice

Why does the sock puppet feel so alone?
Lost in a crevice, it's making a groan.
It twitches and wiggles, giving a shout,
'Who knew this place was a toss-out?'

A dance-off begins with a paperclip,
Each spin and twirl, a delightful trip.
The laughter erupts like a wild kite,
In the nook where misfits find their light.

The Quiet Threshold

At the edge of the world, a door stands clear,
With squeaks and creaks, it whispers near.
It tells a tale of a toad in a hat,
Who dreams of being a fancy diplomat.

So he struts about, with bows and flair,
Offering snacks from his froggy lair.
Frogs and flies, a curious mix,
What treats will he serve? That's the next fix!

Archways of Infinity

In the hall of lost socks, they have a dance,
Spinning and twirling, they take a chance.
One slips and trips, on a lint ball so bright,
And giggles erupt in the soft, moonlight.

With popcorn in hand, the mice gather round,
For tales of the laundry room that astound.
'What's next on the list? A tumble or two?'
The night stretches on with adventures anew.

Liminal Spaces

In the hallway, shoes askew,
A dance of dust bunnies in view.
When the fridge hums a silly tune,
I wonder if it might just swoon.

A cat on the ledge with a pounce,
While the couches quietly bounce.
The clock ticks with a secret thrum,
As snacks giggle and whisper, 'Yum.'

Where Air Meets Stillness

The curtain flutters like a fish,
A breeze, a laugh, and then a swish.
The lamp's light winks, a secret joke,
While shadows dance in playful cloak.

In corners, dust is up to play,
With forgotten socks, a bright bouquet.
Who knew still air could bounce around?
With giggles echoing all around.

The Gap of Uncertainty

A step to the left, a twist of fate,
Where echoes giggle, don't you wait.
In this space where question marks lie,
Do I lock the door, or just try?

From here, the wrong button might beep,
And who knows what secrets to keep?
An umbrella that forgot to close,
Sprays rainbows where no one knows.

Whispered Stories in Transit

The staircase creaks with tales untold,
As dust motes shimmer, brave and bold.
A suitcase chuckles on its ride,
While the floorboards hum a bumpy stride.

In transit, the laughter seems to grow,
As socks pull pranks, then hide and throw.
With each step, adventures sway,
In giggles and whispers, we drift away.

The Cracked Frame of Understanding

In a house of mixed up dreams,
Where nothing's quite as it seems.
A cat plots schemes with a sly grin,
While I search for sanity within.

The milk's gone sour, the toast is burned,
I try to learn but I'm still spurned.
The Wi-Fi signals jump and jive,
In this peculiar little hive.

With socks that vanish, where do they go?
Is there a sock thief in the flow?
Each crack in the frame holds a tale,
A comedy where logic may fail.

So here I laugh at the absurd,
In this circus, reality's blurred.
The frames may crack, but the heart's still keen,
To love the quirks of the unseen.

Murmurs of the Unseen

In the quiet corners of the night,
Whispers chuckle, hiding from sight.
The ghost of a sandwich floats by my head,
With a pickle of wisdom that's finally said.

A shadowed nook, where the secrets play,
With laughter echoing in disarray.
The tick-tock of silence, so loud it seems,
Is filled with giggles of forgotten dreams.

Socks are debating, they're rowdy and bold,
Swapping stories of journeys untold.
While my chair wobbles, trying to stand,
What's real and what's simply unplanned?

With giggles that dance on the breeze,
And inanimate friends at my knees,
I choose to embrace the chaos within,
For in every riddle lies a cheeky grin.

The Boundary of Seen and Unseen

On the border of what we perceive,
Lies a world where oddities cleave.
My plants are chatting, yes, it's true,
Debating the shade of their leafy hue.

Balloons float by, in a merry parade,
With wishes ungranted from years that fade.
They giggle with glee as they drift away,
Leaving me pondering the price to pay.

A squirrel debates with a hapless crow,
Who's the champion of the show?
Each glance in the mirror concedes a prank,
As reality winks with a knowing crank.

In the realm of sight and things concealed,\nEvery glance reveals what's unpeeled.
So here I dwell in the playful quirks,
Where the unseen life jovially lurks.

Fading Light on the Divide

As dusk wraps around with a whimsical breeze,
Muffled laughter sneaks in with ease.
A chicken in sneakers dances on by,
Chasing shadows that tickle the sky.

The lamp flickers like it's lost in thought,
Debating all the wonders it's sought.
While the floorboards creak in a merry tune,
Telling secrets of spoons and a jaunty moon.

In corners where laughter seems to abide,
The blissful mess winks with pride.
A treasure map drawn in crayon and cheer,
In this fading light, no need to adhere.

So join the parade of the odd and unique,
As reality teases with a comic streak.
With each giggle fading into the night,
We embrace the divide, our hearts feel light.

Veils of the Unseen

A cat in a hat thinks it's grand,
It struts like a king, on command.
The dog wears a shoe, one on each paw,
Chasing its tail in a comic flaw.

A squirrel with glasses reads a book,
In search of the secret cheese nook.
The curtains are twitching, oh what a sight,
As the mouse plans a party every night.

The fish in the bowl joins the fun,
With stories of pirates and treasure run.
The things that we miss when we start to stare,
Are the giggles and antics that float in the air.

So lift up the veil and take a peek,
At the laughter that hides in a game of hide-and-seek.

Fleeting Shadows and Silhouettes

The shadows dance with a playful sway,
In the corners where the dust bunnies play.
A broom takes a break, sipping some tea,
While the mop tries to waltz, oh what glee!

A silhouette prances, all lost in the light,
Twisting and turning, it takes to flight.
With a wink and a grin, it vanishes fast,
Leaving echoes of laughter from the past.

The sun plays tricks on the wall with a tease,
Bending and stretching like a cat with ease.
The curtains giggle, swaying left and right,
As night creeps in, dimming the kite.

In this dance of shrouded delight,
A carnival of giggles takes flight.

The Space of Unfolding Stories

In the hall where whispers gather round,
A tale unfolds without a sound.
The chairperson huffs, holding a pen,
As the clock ticks slowly, again and again.

A rug with patterns tells of yore,
While gossiping plants spill tales galore.
The walls lean in, eager to hear,
As secrets unravel, drawing us near.

Pictures hang crooked, full of delight,
Their smiles trapped in a canvas so bright.
They chuckle softly, their stories untold,
In this space where memories unfold.

Each notch in the wood holds a laugh,
In the corners of time, we find our path.

Framed Moments of Solitude

In a frame on the wall, a lone cookie sat,
Winking at crumbs, all covered in fat.
It dreams of the party it missed last week,
With frosting and fun, oh, so bleak!

A lonely sock rolls by, lost in the fray,
On a quest for its pair in an odd ballet.
It twirls and it spins, then finds its stride,
In the corner where mismatched things often hide.

With a sniffle and giggle, a bubble takes flight,
Catching the rays of the soft evening light.
It floats without care, a whimsical sight,
In the quiet of moments, when we feel just right.

So here in this space, humor unfolds,
In frames of solitude where laughter holds.

Fleeting Moments in the Crack

In a crack where the sunlight peeks,
A squirrel thinks he's got his cheeks.
He hoards his acorns with such pride,
While birds just laugh from the inside.

A dance of shadows, a quick little show,
The breeze makes laughs, and time does slow.
A cat might leap, but slips instead,
It's comedy gold, much to be said.

The ants march by, in perfect line,
With tiny briefcases that look so fine.
They gossip about the grass so green,
In the crack where silliness reigns supreme.

A distant sound, a door will creak,
The world outside seems far from bleak.
In this tiny space, chaos goes wild,
Fleeting moments make the child reviled.

The Intersection of Dreams

At the corner seat, where wishes meet,
A toaster dreams of dancing feet.
Jam and bread, they sway in tune,
In perfect harmony, beneath the moon.

A sock fights back from the dryer's fate,
It's lost its mate, but no time to wait.
With goofy hops and silly spins,
It starts a party; the fun begins!

A pillow whispers sweet nothings near,
To an old shoe that drinks its beer.
They laugh about the things they've seen,
In twilight's glow, they giggle and preen.

When stars align and dreams collide,
A world of humor is amplified.
In this whimsical realm of night,
Life's absurdity feels just right.

A Breath of Mystery

There's a whisper from the beans that brew,
A curious tale, once known by few.
The coffee pot sings as it bubbles away,
While muffins chuckle, as if to say!

Old books sit, on a shelf so high,
Each one holds secrets, but none will lie.
They tell of worlds where laughter reigns,
And silly moments that tickle the brains.

A ghost in the attic, with socks askew,
Turns cartwheels for the eager crew.
He shouts out jokes with a foggy twirl,
Making the night spin and whirl.

In this haze of absurd delight,
Make room for giggles that dance in flight.
A breath of mystery in every rhyme,
Funny little thoughts that defy time.

The Edge of Echoes

At the edge where echoes delight,
A lizard basks in the warm twilight.
It tells tales of flies and friendly frowns,
While nearby, a clown performs in crowns.

The laughter ripples with every sound,
As a leaf tumbles gently to the ground.
A joke however old can feel brand new,
When whispered softly, it draws a crew.

In corners where shadows play peek-a-boo,
A mischievous breeze has its fun too.
It tangles the hair of a passing chap,
Who laughs and sways, falling with a flap.

Each call and response adds to the cheer,
With echoes that shimmer, drawing us near.
A world of whimsy found here to roam,
In this laughter-filled place we call home.

Echoes of Unseen Passages

A shadow danced on the carpet,
While the cat was planning a heist.
My socks, it seemed, had vanished,
Caught in a game of 'who's the least nice.'

The hallway whispers in secret,
A breeze plays tricks on my hair.
Is it ghosts or my own two feet,
That make me question my own flair?

The lamp flickers—was that a signal?
Time for a party with ghosts to attend.
I tiptoe around in my slippers,
Pretending I've got it all planned out, my friend.

With each odd creak of the floorboards,
A giggle bursts forth from thin air.
Who knew this house had a sense of humor,
Inviting chaos, but not a care?

The Veil of Uncertainty

A sneeze echoes through the hallway,
Am I alone or just insane?
The curtains flutter, mischievous,
I swear they're laughing at my pain.

Each corner hides a riddle,
With hats and shoes askew on the floor.
Did I leave the fridge open again?
Or is that just my mind going for more?

The fridge hums a catchy tune,
Daring me to make a snack.
But in my quest for late-night munchies,
I trip on a shoe, what a whack!

In this maze of endless wonder,
Every step's a slapstick feat.
Who knew life would be this funny,
With the mundane playing tricks on my feet?

Whispered Possibilities

A knock at the wall, who can it be?
The broom has secrets, or so it seems.
With a wink and a swish, it's looming near,
Ready to stir up my wildest dreams.

The picture frames giggle in silence,
While I ponder where I left my keys.
They're lost, not stolen, just misplaced,
To a land of whimsical antics and tease.

A pillow fight breaks out, oh dear!
As laughter drowns out my wary thoughts.
Each feather that flies is a memory,
Covering the chaos that life has brought.

In this drama of the mundane,
I toss my cares to the side.
For even the mess of my living space,
Can turn the dull day into a wild ride!

Framed by Light and Shadow

The lamp casts a glow like a spotlight,
As I juggle my breakfast with flair.
Toast may fly, and the jam could splat,
But honestly, who needs a repair?

My coffee's a untamed river,
Flowing over the rim with glee.
It tells me the morning has started,
With humor and spills, oh look at me!

In a corner, a clock rolls its eyes,
Tick-tocking jokes that I can't grasp.
Each minute teases my patience, oh my,
I laugh with each second I can't clasp.

With shadows that stretch to infinity,
I dance in chaotic delight.
For life's little jests are magnificent,
As I frolic through morning's soft light.

Duality in the Silence

There's a knock, then a pause,
I pretend not to hear,
The pizza's running late,
Or maybe it's the fear.

Two whispers dance around,
One's right, one's a lie,
In this quiet chaos,
Why do my thoughts fly?

Should I let them in fast,
Or just hide and be sly?
The knocking starts again,
I think I'll just cry.

As they flee down the hall,
I start to feel free.
I've learned quite a lot,
Sometimes two's just a spree.

In the Shadow of Perceptions

A shadow thinks it's bold,
But it's just light's refrain,
Dancing awkwardly now,
   Like a duck on a train.

Squirrels wave from the leads,
   Telling secrets to air,
While I'm lost in my thoughts,
   Wondering if they care.

Peeking out from my chair,
   I see two tigers prance.
One's fierce, one's just fluff,
   Oh, what a wild dance!

Through the crack I could yell,
   But who would really hear?
   Even shadows get tired,
   Of their own little cheer.

Through the Grille of Hope

I watched through the holes,
A parade of lost socks,
Tiptoeing on the grass,
And hiding from clocks.

They wiggled and jiggled,
All shapes and some stains,
Competing for my heart,
In this game of refrains.

With a wink and a flap,
They danced towards the light,
My hope's just a sock,
That's lost in plain sight.

I chuckled and sighed,
What a peculiar show!
Life's circus continues,
With no tickets to show.

The Gate of Perceptions

I found a gate ajar,
It squeaked like a cat,
Peeking just for fun,
To see where it's at.

A rabbit hopped on by,
Wearing glasses, quite sly,
It turned, gave a wink,
Then whispered a lie.

Behind the gate was gold,
Or maybe it was fluff?
My mind had a picture,
Now I'm just too gruff.

With a dash and a hop,
I chose to retreat,
From the antics of gates,
And my own quick defeat.

Threshold Reveries

A foot in both worlds, I dance and prance,
A world of chaos, with a hint of chance.
Every creak and groan, a joke to unfold,
In this silly limbo, brave and bold.

The cat rolls over, in fits of pure glee,
Chasing shadows, thinking they're free.
While a sock's on the floor, plotting its fate,
Will it end up in laundry or stuck on a plate?

A doorbell rings, but it's just a prank,
With no one outside but the neighbor's tank.
I leap to the left — oh wait, what a sight!
That door just closed — what a wonderful fright!

With humor in space, and laughter's embrace,
I twirl on the threshold, a marvelous place.
In this land of the silly, where dreams like to play,
I giggle and wiggle, come join my ballet!

Shadows at the Crossroad

At the crossroad, where shadows tease,
I meet a squirrel with plans to squeeze.
He whispers "Choose left, or you may regret,"
But what if straight leads to a fishnet?

Two paths diverge, oh what a delight!
One's full of laughter, the other, a fright.
I take a step, and what do I see?
Timmy the turtle just mocking me.

"Choose wisely!" he quips with a chuckle so grand,
While juggling conch shells, just as he planned.
But which way to go? The dilemma's quite real,
The left leads to pie, the right to a wheel!

So I shimmy and shake, with decision made,
I leap to the left, my worries now weighed.
For humor and joy, in twilight's soft hold,
Turn shadows to laughter, be brave and be bold.

Glimpses of Twilight

As twilight descends, the light starts to fade,
I dance like a puppet, both foolish and played.
The tree outside chuckles, a grin on its bark,
And I trip over roots, in this laughter-filled park.

With each brush of dusk, the fireflies spring,
Their flashes like jokes—oh, the joy that they bring!
I chase after mirth in a whimsical race,
But stumble on shadows that hide with a trace.

Panels of laughter, floating in midair,
As the moonlight pokes fun, without any care.
And who should appear but a wise old crow,
With riddles and rhymes, and plenty of show!

In the twilight's embrace, I find my sweet grace,
For every misstep becomes a face-palm trace.
So I giggle and wiggle, in this fading light,
Between chuckles and dreams, all feels just right!

The Space Where Secrets Linger

In a space where secrets flit and fly,
I spy a broomstick with a wink in its eye.
"Let's stir up some trouble," it silently fraught,
While a rolling pin plots out what it has sought.

A whispering wall, it holds tight its lore,
Of crumbs that escaped, and an open back door.
The toaster's hot tales, it pops up with glee,
Could electricity cause giggles in tea?

Behind cupboard doors, where the old things reside,
Dust bunnies chuckle, side by side they abide.
They're stockpiling tales of socks lost in time,
As they dance on the floor, and begin to rhyme.

So step with a smile, in this humorous haze,
Where laughter and secrets weave playful displays.
In a world of the odd, let your heart take the lead,
As joy fills the gaps, and you're always freed!

Portals of Imagination

In a world where socks take flight,
And toasters dance under moonlight,
A cat wearing boots gives a wink,
As goldfish plot with a wink.

The chair insists it's a swan,
While the hat claims it's a brawn,
Lollipop trees grow on the floor,
And candy clouds knock on your door.

But when you peek through the frames,
A chorus of broccoli sings names,
Bouncing on trampolines made of cheese,
Inviting you to join with ease.

In this land of frolic and glee,
Every shadow shakes off its spree,
So tiptoe through laughter's embrace,
And leave with a smile on your face.

Echoes of Distant Dreams

There's a penguin dressed as a knight,
Sipping tea under a disco light,
Balloons float past in a parade,
Each one a tale that's never made.

A whispering rug tells a joke,
As the ceiling laughs and nearly chokes,
The clock skips beats with quirky grace,
While lightning bugs find their own pace.

Swings made of spaghetti sway,
While rainbows hang out for the day,
The moon wears shades in a bright suit,
And clowns ride bikes that honk and toot.

So chase those echoes as they gleam,
In a twilight space of every dream,
For laughter stitches each missed chance,
In this merry, cosmic dance.

The Lattice of Perception

A banana peels back to say,
'Let's start a game of hide and sway!',
As a parrot draws a heat map,
Of where to find a cozy nap.

On tippy toes, the fridge has style,
It opens wide with a cheeky smile,
Helping milk to do the cha-cha,
While carrots clink like a fervent raga.

Walls giggle with a paintbrush stroke,
Creating paths where shadows joke,
The sun wears a hat just for fun,
As plastic cups bask in the sun.

Embrace the whimsy on this ride,
Where everything has art inside,
So break the rules, flip the page,
And laugh out loud from your own stage.

Whispers from the Other Side

A squirrel in a cape takes a leap,
Whispering secrets the sun can keep,
While clouds hold meetings of silly kinds,
Discussing the world through cottony minds.

Fish wearing hats tap-dance in streams,
While dishes discuss their wildest dreams,
And the moon spins tales of painted skies,
Starring the stars in a cheeky guise.

A light bulb juggles ideas with ease,
As shadows stretch and sway like trees,
The wind plays hopscotch on the grass,
Making laughter through moments that pass.

So open your heart to absurdity's grace,
And let joy skip with a playful pace,
For the whispers echo in playful glee,
On the other side of reality.

When Walls Hold Breath

In the hallway's playful sway,
Walls whisper secrets of ballet.
A cat meows, then takes a leap,
While shadows dance, a comical sweep.

The fridge hums a cheerful tune,
As if it's holding back a balloon.
Cactus grins, a prickly sage,
Sharing jokes on a lively stage.

Curtains flutter in glee and jest,
As daylight plays its jeopardy quest.
A sock takes flight, lost in a whirl,
While the lamp giggles, unbending, unfurl.

Here laughter echoes in painted walls,
Twisting tales as humor calls.
With every step, a jest unfolds,
As light and shadow share their golds.

The Ambiguity of Entry

Footsteps shuffle, a grand parade,
Knocking on doors where none are laid.
A clown hat sits atop a chair,
Who's the guest? Do we even care?

A curtain swings, then stops mid-swing,
While emptiness starts to sing.
A doorknob laughs, spinning round,
Signaling adventures yet unfound.

The key is lost, but what a find!
Invention blooms within the mind.
Do we step in or step away?
A riddle plays through night and day.

Echoes of giggles fill the space,
Dare we take on life's little race?
In uncertainty, joy arises,
Finding fun in puzzling prizes.

Reflections in a Silent Frame

Mirrors chuckle, they love a jest,
In their stillness, they never rest.
A smudge of lipstick makes us grin,
As we wonder just where to begin.

Footprints blur, slipping from sight,
As we ponder the nature of light.
A sweater laughs, full of fluff,
As it teases the dog, soft and tough.

Pondering moments flash like a spark,
In a world where the odd leaves its mark.
A wink from the vase, a nod from the chair,
In this quiet, life's gags fill the air.

Twirling thoughts take a vivid leap,
While the clock ticks, but it doesn't keep.
In frames of silence, giggles ring true,
As reflections dance just for you.

The Liminal Horizon

Dancing at the edge of day,
Where silliness is free to play.
A puppy chases a tail it can't catch,
In this funny world full of mismatched.

Steps that pause, then take a chance,
In this space, find your silly dance.
Gravity giggles as a feather floats,
While laughter bounces in rainbow boats.

Sunsets linger, teasing the night,
Colors swirl in a comical fight.
Across the threshold, jesters hide,
Inviting all for a whimsical ride.

The horizon laughs as we draw near,
Every step brings the silly cheer.
In limbo's grasp, we twirl and spin,
Finding joy in the midst of the in.

Between Reflections and Reality

In a mirror with a wink, it said,
"Who is that silly grin, instead?"
A face trying to fit in tight,
But not quite right—oh, what a sight!

Flipping pancakes while I prance,
With butter dreams, I take a chance.
But in the mirror, I must say,
The pancakes laugh and dance away!

The Crossroads of Views

At the fork, I lost my shoe,
One side says 'Go!', the other 'Boo!'
A squirrel laughs from the old oak tree,
'Choose wisely, friend! We've got to flee!'

A sign reads 'Nowhere', with a twist,
I picked the path that's hard to miss.
But every step brings me surprise,
And shows me lessons in all the lies!

The Portal of Potential

This door claims to lead to fate,
But not without a twist of late.
On the other side, I hear some cheers,
Or are they giggles, filled with jeers?

I open wide and step with flair,
And find a world of cushions there!
Where every blunder is a laugh,
And I become the richest half!

Sights Unshared

Here's a view of socks gone rogue,
One with stripes, the other a fog.
They dance around my kitchen floor,
As if they're staging a sock encore!

And in the fridge, a lonely pear,
With tales of journeys, none to share.
It whispers soft in fruity rhymes,
Of visions lost in lunch break crimes!

Spaces Unbound

In a room where socks go to hide,
The toaster plays a game of pride.
The fridge whispers secrets to the cat,
While the plants gossip, imagine that!

Chairs waltz when no one's aware,
Cushions leap without a care.
A vacuum dances with a broom,
In this nonsensical little room!

Echoes bounce off the creaky floor,
As curtains peek, oh what a score!
The clock ticks to a quirky beat,
While dust bunnies shake their feet!

Under the rug, sneaky things dwell,
Counting the stories they won't tell.
A realm of laughter, absurd delight,
Where every object jokes at night!

The Imaginary Threshold

There's a line that wanders, takes its own path,
Daring the lost to engage in a laugh.
Do we step or do we hop?
Both options lead to a comic drop!

A door creaks open with a grin,
Inviting us into a world of sin.
'Welcome!' it says, 'with wiggles and giggles,
We serve the finest of squishy squiggles!'

On the sill, a frog wears a hat,
Ribbiting proudly at the spat.
A mouse performs ballet with flair,
While the broom just watches, too shy to dare!

Here we can leap into thin air,
Where clouds wear shoes and have no care.
Beyond this threshold of giggling jest,
Lies a world that's simply the best!

Glances from the Periphery

From the corner of eyes, things may creep,
Whispers of jokes that never sleep.
An old shoe dances alone in the hall,
While apples debate which one is tall!

A mischievous mouse with a wink,
Offers cheese as we pause to think.
Windows grin, frames almost chat,
As shadows throw confetti like that!

Eavesdropping laughter from behind the potted plant,
Telling tales that riddle and chant.
A vacuum snickers, 'I'll clean your mess!'
While socks on the floor tease with finesse!

Cactus plants in a bubble bath,
Planning their next mischievous path.
Every glance a new twist, a surprise,
In this array, where humor lies!

Beyond the Sightline

What spritz of whimsy lingers near?
The teapot chuckles, oh so dear!
Beyond the edge of what we see,
Imagination loves to roam free.

A bookcase leans in for a peek,
The stories whisper, the spines speak.
Beyond the shelf, a cereal box,
Confides its dreams of breakdancing socks!

Under the stairs, the shadows convene,
Spilling stories, absurd and keen.
A moonbeam twirls, a silly dance,
As the old rubber band joins in with a glance!

Tales of socks and skippers abound,
Where echoes of giggles swirl around.
Each cue to chuckle, an unseen sign,
In this realm, all things intertwine!

Dilemmas of Glass and Grain

I stood and stared at shiny panes,
My thoughts got lost in silly chains.
Should I knock or should I wave?
The grain of wood said, "Be brave!"

A squirrel peeked with a twitchy tail,
I pondered long, began to flail.
Glass sparkled bright, a siren's call,
Is this a party? Should I crawl?

The door creaked slow, a ghostly tease,
Laughter floated in the breeze.
I sighed and thought, with humor spry,
What if it's a clown in disguise?

In friendly jest, I made my stance,
Would they laugh or give a glance?
For in this space of mixed-up play,
Do I step in or walk away?

A Footstep into the Unknown

One foot in chaos, one in the calm,
I paused to breathe, my inner balm.
The hallway twisted in mock delight,
Should I tiptoe or charge outright?

A cat sat there in oversized shoes,
It winked at me like it knew the blues.
With one big leap, I took my chance,
And almost tripped on the cat's dance!

The floorboard squeaked, a funny sound,
A ghostly whisper danced around.
"Hello!" I yelled, but none replied,
Just echoes spun from side to side.

Oh, what a mess in this quirky space,
Each step a riddle, a game to chase.
With giggles rolling like summer waves,
I found my joy in the path it paves.

Murmurs from the Threshold

On the edge of something, I twirled my fate,
A ticklish breeze said, "Come, don't wait!"
Voices bubbled from thin air,
"Don't be shy, come join the dare!"

Peeking through where shadows blend,
I wondered where all this might end.
A party? A prank? Or just some ghouls?
I braved the whispers—after all, who rules?

Tick-tock, tick-tock, what could go wrong?
Maybe a jester, or a weird song.
Yet laughter echoed, and I felt bold,
This threshold promised a tale retold.

So with a grin, I crossed the line,
Into the chuckles, the chaos divine.
With every step, I found my cheer,
Murmurs turned to laughter, crystal clear!

Cerulean Space Between

In a pocket of air, colors collide,
Bluish hues where secrets hide.
I floated there with a goofy grin,
What lay beyond? Should I dive in?

The walls were painted with silly swirls,
A dance of laughter, a twist that twirls.
Should I engage, or simply sway?
These colors beckon with bright ballet.

A parrot squawked from afar,
"Don't be shy, be a bright star!"
In this cerulean stretch of day,
A game unfolded, come what may.

So I leapt into the vibrant hue,
With a wink at the parrot, I bid adieu.
In this silly space where dreams ignite,
Every step sparked joy, oh what delight!

Unspoken Boundaries

There's a sign that says, "Do Not Enter,"
Yet here I am, a sneaky center.
I tiptoe past with comic care,
Spying on squirrels without a scare.

My neighbor's cat gives me a stare,
As if attending to my affair.
I whisper secrets to the breeze,
Sharing laughs with the silly trees.

In the gap, the world feels bright,
What's wrong with this unusual sight?
A dance of shadows, a playful tease,
I play the fool with this cool breeze.

A fence divides, but who's to know?
I hop and skip with ecstatic flow.
They say it's serious, so refined,
But I'm just here, hilariously blind.

Moments Caught in Glass

Reflections giggle with a wink,
Glass panes capture more than we think.
I see my hair going awry,
A fashionable mess, oh my, oh my!

My coffee spills at the window's edge,
A dance of chaos, a clumsy pledge.
The froth creates a joyful splash,
My laugh's so loud, I make a crash.

Passersby chuckle, shaking their heads,
As I juggle mugs, to coffee I'm wed.
An unplanned show, such a delight,
From behind the glass, my greatest plight.

Every moment caught, a memory blends,
Through foggy panes, the laughter extends.
Trapped in this frame, what a sight to see,
Life's messy moments, just the way to be!

The Edge of Two Worlds

On the line where two sides meet,
I balance here on my own two feet.
One leg in the grass, one in the mud,
Like a goat who missed the perfect stud.

The birds argue which side is best,
I'm the referee, a curious jest.
"Are we wild? Or refined today?"
I shout, as chaos dances in play.

Here dogs chase cats, what a spectacle,
While I sip juice, feeling respectable.
The sun and shade take turns to tease,
I'm half-wild, half-serious—what a breeze!

Two worlds collide, laughter erupts,
I stand here in bliss, while chaos disrupts.
At this boundary, I can't be confined,
My inner goofball's perfectly aligned!

Reflections in the Divide

Mirrors show all, the truth's on display,
Each side gives giggles, in its own way.
I wave at myself with a silly grin,
Who knew the fun could bubble from within?

A squirrel peeks in, curious too,
What's happening here in this weird view?
I pull funny faces, we share a laugh,
My reflection a jester, a comical math.

The grass is greener, the joke's on me,
Stuck in this limbo, fancy-free.
I dance to the tune of an unseen band,
Life's little quirks, oh, isn't it grand?

With the divide, the mischief flows,
In each reflection, oh how it grows.
So here I stand, in laughter I abide,
In this whimsical world, where joy's multiplied!

A Gaze from the Overlook

From high above, I peer down low,
Two worlds collide, a comic show.
The cat in a hat, the dog in shoes,
Both take their turns, a tango of blues.

The squirrel stares, with eyes so wide,
Wondering what's on the other side.
A look, a wink, a silent cheer,
All at once, everything seems clear.

A pie flies by, just out of reach,
Caught in the air, like a bad speech.
A grin spreads on my face, so fine,
As chaos dances on a thin line.

Laughter echoes through the trees,
With antics like these, life's a breeze.
Joint mischief, puns in flight,
Who knew odd views could bring such light?

The Uncharted Divide

In a realm where socks mismatched roam,
One side is cozy, the other a foam.
A garden gnome dressed up for a ball,
Wonders why no one's here at all.

The grass is greener, but oh so fake,
"Is that a cake or just a mistake?"
A butterfly whispers, "What's the plan?"
As everyone joins, a quirky clan.

An argument brews 'bout which way to tread,
"Left to the pizza, or right with dread?"
With giggles in tow, they bicker and tease,
Each path promising infinite cheese.

In sticky situations, confusion dwells,
With jokes that ring like silly bells.
This divide, though strange, draws a grin,
Turn mishaps to laughter, let the fun begin!

Paths of Transition

Over the fence, I see three ways,
With dancing creatures and silly plays.
A rabbit wearing glasses, trying to read,
Gives a nod to a chicken, who's off with speed.

A line of ants form a conga line,
While a turtle can't keep pace, yet feels fine.
Between shadows, they play hide and seek,
With giggles that echo, they all feel unique.

A forgotten shoe becomes a throne,
While the crow caws, "Come join my zone!"
Each step forward makes them laugh out loud,
And they'd make the strangest of all crowds.

Transformation lives in the silliest act,
For what seems awkward might be just a fact.
In this odd assembly, life feels sublime,
With the path of laughter set to climb.

Air of Suspended Time

Tick-tock, tick-tock, the clock just froze,
A snail asks, "Where'd the swift time go?"
With a wink from a lizard playing the flute,
The world pauses mid-step, in absolute loot.

The dog rolls by, in perfect slow motion,
Chasing a ball through a wild commotion.
A squirrel's leap hangs, like a momentary pause,
He contemplates acorns with wily applause.

Wandering through space, a butterfly grins,
"Time can't catch up with my quick spins!"
Each second stretched to a giggly delight,
As laughter echoes in this enchanted night.

In this universe where nothing gets done,
The pause makes it clear—life's all about fun.
With every heartbeat, craziness chimes,
In the air of nonsense, we dance through rhymes.

The Veil of Glimpses

In snippets of vision, I stare,
A squirrel sneaks past, oh, where?
A cat's tail twitches, plotting fun,
While sunlight dances, laughing on the run.

Someone's shoehorn, what a find!
Perhaps in Bermuda, roaming blind?
Or just another sock on vacation,
Snuggled up, seeking admiration?

A bird takes a sip, a cartoon spree,
While pigeons debate their own decree.
Laughter echoes through the vine,
Chasing each glimpse, feeling so divine.

So peep through the curtain, join the ride,
In this comedy show, there's nothing to hide.
With every glance, the world unfolds,
A hilarious tale, just waiting to be told.

Shadows in the Aperture

A shadow wobbles, giddy and spry,
With dance moves peculiar, oh my!
Caught in a moment, it trips on a shoe,
A silent movie, but still feels like a zoo.

The cat gives chase, but not very far,
Suddenly distracted, thanks to a car.
A squirrel above watches, munching away,
Judging the chaos, just another day.

The light flickers, changing the scene,
As the shadows play their tricks so mean.
Twisting and turning, they laugh and they writhe,
In this odd little world, the oddness thrives.

Stare through the crack, don't miss a scene,
In the light and the dark, there's always a glean.
What fun it is, this playful ballet,
A shadowy romp to brighten the gray.

Fragments of a Secret Journey

A suitcase bursts with snacks and delight,
Leaving crumbs strewn from day into night.
Rubber ducks float in an imaginary sea,
On this odd voyage, just you and me.

With jellybeans as currency, we trade,
An adventure unfolds, plans renegade.
Chocolate rivers and licorice trees,
Giggles erupt on the playful breeze.

Maps made of napkins, scribbles untold,
Leading to treasures not bought but sold.
In search of laughter, we wander afar,
As dreams and mischief guide us like a star.

So join the quest, grab a goofy hat,
Tails of giggles and sorrows spat.
In this fragment of time, we boldly embark,
A journey unplanned, a wild remark.

The Realm of Half-Seen

In this jesting realm, what's hiding nearby?
A half-seen giggle, a wiggly sigh.
Mysteries lurking behind a slick pane,
Where socks plan escapes in a comical lane.

A spoon plots a heist from a kitchen brigade,
While forks play poker in a shining façade.
Mugs conspire over coffee-filled dreams,
Creating mischief in ever-wilder schemes.

Blurs of laughter swirl in a dance,
As curtains sway, finding their chance.
This quirky domain is a laugh riot,
Join the mayhem, it's pure joy, try it!

Open your eyes to the absurdity there,
Strange visions that float in the playful air.
Each half-seen moment, a joke to behold,
In this whimsical sphere, secrets unfold.

Explorations in the Half-Light

In the hallway, shadows play,
I trip on shoes, they laugh away.
The cat's my guide, with eyes that gleam,
Is this life real, or just a dream?

A door creaks wide, a ghostly grin,
I poke my head, then rush back in.
The fridge hums tales of snacks undone,
Why's it always food that wins the fun?

Whispers flutter, then quickly fade,
Socks on the floor, a grand parade.
I step through curtains, peek and peek,
What lies ahead? A game of hide and seek.

So here I stand, in giggles caught,
In the space that time forgot.
With every creak, the mischief grows,
In this funny place where nobody knows.

Flickers of Transition

A light flickers, the room it shakes,
I dance with shadows, oh, the mistakes!
The sofa sighs as I plop down,
What's that sound? It's the wonky crown.

My fridge's door swings wide like a sail,
I meet the leftover pizza, it's the holy grail.
The window's view, a bird's fierce stare,
Not my fault if I spilled my hair.

Chasing reflections, I bounce to and fro,
The lamp's a star, putting on a show.
As socks unite in a whirlpool fetch,
Who knew cloth could cause such a sketch?

With giggles echoing, I take my flight,
Caught in the dance of day and night.
In this realm of silly delight,
It's fun to play, until it's bright!

The In-between State

I'm lost in a space, not here nor there,
Peeking out windows, with mischief to share.
My pants are inside-out, oh what a sight,
Unruly fashion, or just pure fright?

I strut round the room like I own the place,
A sock on my head, who needs grace?
The doorbell rings, I freeze in surprise,
It's just the reflection, oh what a prize!

To leap or to linger, my thoughts in a knot,
The vacuum's alive, or so it's not.
An adventure awaits in this quirky zone,
With each spin and leap, I'm far from alone.

So here I giggle, in clumsy ballet,
The weirdness of life leads the way.
In an odd little world, where echoes dance,
Mishaps abound, oh what a chance!

Venturing into Stillness

In stillness I stand, a curious sight,
The clock ticks louder, oh what a fright!
Dust bunnies gather to hold a ball,
Should I join in, or just learn to crawl?

The rug trips me, it's plotting for fun,
A tumble that brings out the silly run.
What's lurking behind a swinging door?
A pile of laundry, oh, such a chore!

From chair to table, I make my roam,
Each step echoes, feels like a poem.
The window's sly grin, I flash a grin back,
In this odd space, I never lack.

So let the stillness sing its song,
In this kooky space, nothing feels wrong.
With laughter and winks, let's take our place,
In this whimsical dance of time and space.

Framed Whispers

In the hall, I spy a sock,
Hiding there, like a shy clock.
A pair mismatched, or so it seems,
Do they whisper of silly dreams?

Laughter spills from hidden cracks,
As the cat dashes, tail attacks.
With a chirp and a twist of fate,
I ponder if it's time to wait.

A ghostly drink has found a spot,
Where mischief brews, we've got a plot.
The rug slips down, a silent shout,
Only giggles from the air scout.

Amidst the quiet, a squeaky floor,
The pitter-patter, I can't ignore.
A moment here, an echo stirs,
Framed whispers dance, oh how it purrs!

Beyond the Frame

Outside the frame, a squirrel prances,
In circles grand, it takes its chances.
With acorns plucked, it snickers bold,
A tale of mischief surely told.

A breeze blows through the painted glass,
Winking eyes, how the moments pass.
It sees me peeking, what a show!
With tiny leaps, it steals the glow.

Cup of tea and a scatter of crumbs,
The cheeky sneaks, such little chums.
They plot and plan, a daring feat,
While I just grin, future's sweet.

A dance of shadows, a robber's cheer,
Amusement found in things so near.
Beyond the frame, the fun persists,
Life's a jest, with twists and twists.

Where Light Meets the Latch

Sunbeam tickles at the latch,
It's time for fun, let's make a match!
A wobbly chair, a bounce, a twist,
Together we'll share a silly tryst.

Through the crack, a breeze does creep,
And straight away, the curtains leap.
Do you hear that? A flurry of sighs,
As daylight jests and moonlight cries.

Kites fly high, chasing the clouds,
While grinning kittens gather crowds.
With a wiggle and a giggle, we tease,
Sprinkling laughter just like confetti trees.

A peep, a poke, what's that I spy?
A cheeky fellow, with a sly eye.
Where light meets the latch, hearts grow bold,
In this world of levity, stories unfold.

Echoes of a Quiet Passage

In the corridor, a whispering air,
Dances and flutters without a care.
What's that? A shoe's misplaced ballet,
Socks in a tiff, much to their dismay!

Laughter trapped in creaky seams,
As the hallways giggle with giddy dreams.
Mouse-sized cheerleaders cheer in delight,
While old chairs creak at this funny sight.

A tick-tock clock with secrets untold,
Chimes a song that never grows old.
Though shadows may linger through twilight's call,
The echoes of jest still capture it all.

In a quiet passage, silliness reigns,
A scene of chaos, where joy sustains.
Each moment dances, paintings alive,
In the hush of the day, funny vibes thrive!

Gazing Through the Lattice

I spy on the squirrels with glee,
They chat in code, just like me.
A nut thief darts, oh what a sight,
While I sip my tea with delight.

The bees buzz by in a merry dance,
Hovering close, they seem to prance.
I wave at them, they wave right back,
In this world, there's nothing I lack.

A cat walks by with a regal air,
She flicks her tail without a care.
From my seat, I'll cheer and shout,
"Hey, Miss Kitty! What's that about?"

The world outside is quite a show,
So much joy from my cozy low.
With laughter swirling in the breeze,
I'm grateful for such little tease.

Mysteries in the Margins

I found a sock stuck in the crack,
Surely it has some tales to unpack.
Whose foot, I wonder, did it adorn?
Did it leap away just out of scorn?

The dust bunnies plot, I can just tell,
Conspiring quietly, all is quite well.
They giggle and tumble, oh what a scene,
Bringing laughter where none has been.

A cardboard box holds treasures galore,
Old photos of friends who are no more.
With each silly smile, I chuckle aloud,
Remembering times that made me proud.

In this nook, odd things find their way,
As laughter mingles with light of day.
The margins are filled with delightful quirks,
Where humor and memory forever lurks.

Where the Heart Peers

A peep through the shutters brings me delight,
Two gnomes in a tussle, what a sight!
They jostle and poke with a mischievous grin,
I can't help but chuckle, where do I begin?

The neighbor's dog has won the race,
He trips on his leash, oh, what a face!
I cheer him on with an enthusiastic bark,
While he stumbles about like a comedy spark.

A pigeon waddles as if to declare,
That life is absurd, and it doesn't care.
With each fluffed feather and strut so bold,
There's laughter in moments that simply unfold.

When clouds drift by, what tales they tell,
Of whimsical creatures who dance very well.
Peering through life, I keep it light,
Where the heart giggles and everything's bright.

The Limits of Visibility

Through frosted glass, I can't quite see,
But I hear the laughter, wild and free.
An echo of joy from outside below,
A party of critters, put on a show!

Five frogs in hats hop to and fro,
To the beat of a tune only they know.
They juggle the flies with whimsical flair,
While I chuckle softly from my comfy chair.

A raccoon peeks in, oh what a tease,
With a glint in his eye, he's sure to please.
He sips from my cup, a rascally thief,
And I can't help but laugh at this silly mischief.

Visibility's tricky, but I won't complain,
For laughter finds ways to break through the rain.
In the bounds of joy where silliness thrives,
I'll cherish these moments, where laughter survives.

Through Fractured Perspectives

A squirrel's dance on the lawn,
Chasing shadows at dawn.
Peering through glass so clear,
Is it madness or just cheer?

A cat's meow, a dog's bark,
As they growl in playful spark.
Through the cracks, we catch a glance,
Of the oddest little dance.

A postman slips, a bike's crash,
Laughter echoes, a bright flash.
Whispers float on sunlight beams,
Reality frays at the seams.

What is truth when jest unfolds?
A world of quirks, yet it holds,
All the absurdity we'll find,
Peering close, we're all entwined.

Glimmers in the Periphery

A twinkle shines in the breeze,
My neighbor's cat climbs with ease.
Perched on the fence, he's so sly,
Catching whispers as they fly.

The kid's scooter upends the trash,
With a clatter, a giggle and crash.
As we peek from our cozy chairs,
Life's little surprises catch stares.

Glances shared with snickers abound,
In this frame, hilarity's found.
Through a lens, we see the jest,
It's all in the angle—what's best?

Moments of joy, little quirks,
The subtle dance of life's works.
In the periphery, we delight,
Finding laughter in plain sight.

The Cloak of Perception

Wearing a hat that's far too tall,
Marvin trips, makes a grand fall.
Laughter bubbles just like a brook,
As he poses with a jesting look.

A breeze tosses leaves in a swirl,
Behind heavy curtains, giggles unfurl.
If you squint hard, you might see it:
Life's a play, and we're all fit.

A dreamer spills soda on his shoe,
In this chaos, there's always a view.
Caught in a tangle, the world spins round,
With a chuckle, we're homeward bound.

Cloaked in humor, we artfully weave,
Moments of joy we choose to believe.
Perception's a trickster, so let it be,
In a world where all sense runs free.

The Gathering of Light

A dance of shadows on faded walls,
Laughter leaps, as the daylight calls.
In silly hats, under sun's bright glee,
The gathering forms like a quirky spree.

A dog in a bowtie, oh what a sight,
Roaming the yard, he's pure delight.
The old bird, with wisdom, takes flight,
While giggles echo, as day turns to night.

Friends gather 'round with snacks on their laps,
Sharing secrets, and silly mishaps.
Every smile brings a spark so bright,
In this moment, everything feels right.

As light fades, the stories entwine,
In the glimmer that dances, we shine.
With laughter shared, we all ignite,
A tapestry woven of joy and light.

Chasing Fleeting Horizons

I sprinted fast to catch a breeze,
But tripped on laces, oh what tease!
A butterfly laughed, fluttering away,
As I landed in a pile of hay.

With every step, the sun did wink,
A dancing shadow made me think.
I reached for dreams that danced ahead,
But bumped my nose instead of tread.

I chased a spark, a glint so bright,
But fell in the mud, oh what a sight!
The horizon giggled, just out of reach,
While I sat grinning, covered in beach.

So here I lie with dreams drawn high,
While ducks just quack and paddle by.
Oh fleeting fun, you're quite the tease,
Let's chase the day with joyful ease.

The Border of Possibilities

In a land where socks never match,
I found a door that made me hatch.
It led to laughter, wide and bright,
Where penguins skated in pure delight.

I tried to sing, my voice went 'boing',
As rubber chickens joined the throng.
With jellybeans raining from the sky,
I wondered if such dreams might fly.

But then I tripped on a shoelace monster,
And landed smack where I'd find a sponsor.
They offered me a job to dance,
But all I did was throw my chance.

So here I stand upon this line,
With socks and dreams that intertwine.
Adventure waits just out of view,
In a land where laughter always feels new.

Fractured Visions

In a world where mirrors seem to lie,
I saw my cat with a tie-up high.
He winked at me, then turned to mold,
While I just laughed, feeling quite bold.

A footstep echoed, oh what a sound,
As clouds wore hats and drifted around.
I blinked twice and what did I see?
A fish in a tux, grinning with glee!

Teapots danced on the ceiling fan,
While I considered my next grand plan.
To step through madness, crack a grin,
And jump in joy for the silliest win.

So here I play with fractured dreams,
And join the dance of silly themes.
For laughter's crown is always near,
In a world spun round with joy and cheer.

A Glimpse Through the Gap

Peeking through that curious crack,
I saw a tune that began to smack.
Dancing jackets with zest galore,
Made me giggle, longing for more.

A rabbit in shorts, what a surprise,
With carrot confetti filling the skies.
I waved my hand, he waved back fast,
Our laughter echoed, such fun unsurpassed!

Frogs in top hats played a refrain,
As I let go of all my mundane.
I tumbled forth with joyful cheers,
And forgot all worries, all my fears.

Oh gap so sly, you tease me so,
With visions of whims and laughter's flow.
For here inside this moment sweet,
I find a world where joy's complete.

The Unseen Passageway

A cat in a hat with a tipple of tea,
Wanders unseen, quite carefree.
In corners it prowls, with a wink and a grin,
Wondering where all the giggles have been.

The shadows play tricks, they giggle and tease,
While mice in their jackets applaud with soft squeaks.
Under the couch, a sock puppet plots,
To overthrow naps and the dust bunnies' shots.

A hidden door swings, but it's merely a joke,
The hinges just creak as we both start to poke.
With a riddle or two, it invites us inside,
To dance with the silliness, no need to hide.

So in this odd realm, we'll hop with delight,
The unseen passageway, oh what a sight!
Not a closet nor hall, but a giggle-filled spree,
Where laughter's the key, it's just you and me.

Floating on the Fringes

A balloon on a string drifted right by,
It floated like whispers from the sky.
With a chuckle, it dipped, teased the ground,
For the silly old cat, who just wanted the sound.

Off to the edges, where dreams come to play,
A schnozzled-up rabbit has something to say.
He hops through the tulips, all tangled and bright,
With jokes about things that give everyone fright.

A gnome in a garden, he rolls with a grin,
Telling tall tales that just might be sin.
In the land of the fancies, where whimsy's the rule,
The fringes are wild; they're charmingly cruel.

"Oh look!" shouts the gnome, "A squirrel in a suit,
Debating with mice who beg for some fruit!"
As laughter erupts in this odd little place,
We float on the fringes, all smiles on our face.

Threshold Dreams

On the edge of the night, as dreams start to bloom,
A jester jigs by with a sly little tune.
He twirls and he spins, a hat five sizes too big,
Singing songs of the sofa's adventures—oh dig!

A sprightly old door, creaky with fate,
Winks at the world, inviting its weight.
As socks start their tango, they slip and they slide,
While pillows bear witness to this giggling ride.

In the realm of the threshold, silliness reigns,
With marshmallow clouds, we'll dance in the lanes.
Laughter is currency, we trade it with cheer,
No worries await us; we've jumped the frontier.

So let's leap through the doorway, let spontaneity soar,
Dreams spark like fireflies, we'll stumble and roar.
With giggles as anchors, we're sailing tonight,
In this wacky embrace, everything feels right.

The Space Where Shadows Dance

In a room where the shadows put on quite a show,
A pirate with polka dots steals the spotlight, oh no!
With a laugh and a swish, he hoists up the sail,
While the lanterns chuckle, as shadows set sail.

A dance of the shadows, all floppy and free,
They wiggle and whirl, so absurdly with glee.
The walls hum a tune, the floor's ready to prance,
As the broom joins the fun, it sweeps with romance.

The corners are crowded, with giggles piled high,
As a lonely old chair starts to glance at the sky.
With a wink and a spin, it joins in the mix,
This space without rules, just laughter's sweet tricks.

So let's revel in night, where joy knows no bounds,
In the space where shadows dance, oh what fun resounds!

With whimsy our guide, we'll twirl until dawn,
In this silly old realm where laughter goes on.

The Jigsaw of Perspective

In a room filled with paintings, so bright and bizarre,
Each frame tells a tale of a life from afar.
Step left to see laughter, step right to see tears,
It's all just a puzzle, aligning our fears.

With faces all squished in a goofy delight,
The art is quite crazy, but oh what a sight!
Can you spot the banana in a hat made of cheese?
It's hard to be serious when you're tickled by these.

A giraffe in a tutu spins circles with glee,
While a penguin in slippers laughs loudly at me.
Each piece of our chatter just adds to the scene,
Like a jigsaw assembled by whispers and screams.

Yet somehow it fits, this madcap collection,
A room full of laughter needs little correction.
So come, grab your corner, let's finish this fun,
In this jigsaw of joy, we are never just one.

Lattice of Choices

A web of decisions hangs thick in the air,
Each thread is a path, which one do we dare?
Should we climb the spaghetti or dive in the pie?
With choices like these, who can tell you why?

There's a fork in the road made of marshmallow fluff,
Where options keep bouncing, it's really quite tough.
Should we skip with a goat or just dance with a cat?
In this lattice of choices, we're all feeling fat!

Can we juggle our dreams like a clown in a hat?
Or hide in a closet with Uncle Bob's cat?
With a laugh and a grin, let's twirl through the mess,
In the lattice we find a delightful excess.

So take a quick peek, what delights lie ahead?
In this playful perplexity, joy doesn't dread!
With each twist and turn, we'll laugh till we drop,
In this lattice of choices, we'll never just stop.

The Quiet Convergence

In the hush of the night, when the clocks seem to giggle,
The stars start to dance and the shadows just wiggle.
Every whisper's a secret, a story to tell,
Where laughter collides in this clumsy carousel.

A meeting of minds in a flicker of light,
They gossip and chuckle, all merry, all bright.
With socks made of kittens and shoes made of cheese,
This quiet convergence brings joy to our knees.

What plans do they hatch in this mystical space?
With flapping of wings and a dash of pure grace.
From the bubbles of chuckles, we all hear the call,
In these moments of magic, let's giggle, let's sprawl!

So join us in silence when laughter takes flight,
In the calm of the night, we'll dream pure delight.
With a wink and a nudge, we'll dance on the breeze,
In this quiet convergence, our hearts feel at ease.

Bridging What Remains

With a grin on our faces, we cross over gaps,
A bridge made of wishes, where silliness claps.
With taffy for railings and gumdrops for glue,
We'll skip to the middle, just me and you.

What's left on the other side? Who really can tell?
It could be a circus or just one big shell.
The map shows a rainbow, the eggs dance around,
In this bridging of dreams, great fortune is found!

With a tiptoe on jelly and a hop on a cloud,
We'll forge a new trail, innovative and loud.
Each step that we take brings a chuckle or two,
What lingers behind us, we can laugh and renew.

Strung out like pasta, our memories gleam,
Holding on to the laughter, we weave through a dream.
So let's bridge what remains with a touch of the zest,
In this silly adventure, we'll always be blessed.

www.ingramcontent.com/pod-product-compliance
Lightning Source LLC
Chambersburg PA
CBHW060117230426
43661CB00003B/224